Little People, BIG DREAMS®
MOTHER TERESA

Written by
Maria Isabel Sánchez Vegara

Illustrated by
Natascha Rosenberg

Frances Lincoln
Children's Books

Once, there was a little Albanian girl who was always willing to give a helping hand. Her name was Agnes, and she lived in Skopje, with her parents and two siblings.

Agnes was raised to love God and love others above all else. Little did she know that in the future she would be known as Saint Teresa of Calcutta...

One day, a new priest arrived in town. He had been working in India, far from where Agnes lived. She loved listening to his stories about helping the poor in the city of Calcutta.

So, when she turned 18, Agnes said goodbye to her family and started a long journey. She was determined to become a nun and help people — no matter what.

She travelled to Ireland and joined the sisters of Loreto.
Once she had settled at the convent, Agnes asked the
nuns to call her 'Teresa' from that day on.

A few months later, she was ready to board a ship and travel to India. The language, the colours, the food, the smells... everything was new and different for her!

Mother Teresa taught at a school for many years. But she knew there were some people who needed her more than her students: the poorest of the poor.

Mother Teresa took to the streets of Calcutta, determined to help the first person in need. She had hardly taken three steps before she stumbled upon a woman who was lying on the ground.

Soon, 12 students joined her. They called themselves the 'Missionaries of Charity' and they set out to care for all those who needed it. They chose to wear a simple sari.

Mother Teresa opened a hospital in an old Hindu temple. There was always one more bed, one more plate of rice, and one more blanket to cover whoever needed it. She knew that the smallest things could make the biggest difference.

For more than twenty years, she picked up thousands of people from the streets of India. She opened hospitals, orphanages and schools all over the world.

She received all the awards that could be given
to a single person. But she only accepted them
in the name of the poor.

Mother Teresa sent a beautiful message out to the world: it doesn't matter if you do big or small things in your life, as long as you do them with great love.

MOTHER TERESA

(Born 1910 • Died 1997)

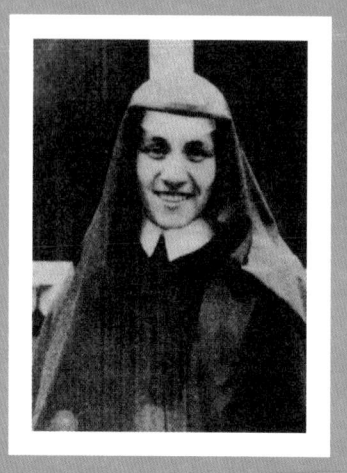

c. 1925 (left)   c. 1930

Anjezë Gonxhe Bojaxhiu was of Albanian descent and born in
Skopje (now the capital of North Macedonia). The Anglicised version
of Anjezë (Agnes) has been used in this book. Agnes lived with
her mother, father, older brother and sister. Her family followed
the Roman Catholic faith, and this could be seen in their everyday
life. Her family weren't rich but opened their home to people who
needed help. Her mother would provide strangers with hot food
and a place to rest. She taught Agnes to see God in the faces of
strangers. At 12, Agnes then heard 'the call' to dedicate her life to
God. Her mother thought she was too young, but the voice persisted
over the next few years. Agnes was fascinated by stories of Catholic

1971   1974

missionaries, people who travelled to faraway places to help those in need. At 18, she set off to join a convent in Ireland, taking her vows as Sister Teresa. She travelled to India to teach at a school in Calcutta, where she became 'Mother Teresa'. Mother Teresa was on a train to Darjeeling when she heard the 'call within the call'. She believed God wanted her to help the poor whilst living among them. She founded the 'Missionaries of Charity' and many nuns joined her. They set up hospitals, comforted the sick and cared for the poor when no-one else did. She was awarded the Nobel Peace Prize in 1979 for her work. After she died, she was awarded a sainthood by Pope Francis in 2015. The Missionaries of Charity still continue Saint Teresa's work today.

Want to find out more about **Mother Teresa?**
Have a read of these great books:

Who Was Mother Teresa? by Jim Gigliotti and David Groff
DK Biography: Mother Teresa by Maya Gold
Mother Teresa: The Life of Mother Teresa by Paul Harrison

You can read more about the work of the Missionaries of Charity, on their
website: 'The Mother Teresa of Calcutta Centre'.

Brimming with creative inspiration, how-to projects, and useful
information to enrich your everyday life, Quarto Knows is a favourite
destination for those pursuing their interests and passions. Visit our
site and dig deeper with our books into your area of interest:
Quarto Creates, Quarto Cooks, Quarto Homes, Quarto Lives,
Quarto Drives, Quarto Explores, Quarto Gifts, or Quarto Kids.

Text copyright © 2018 Maria Isabel Sánchez Vegara. Illustrations copyright © 2018 Natascha Rosenberg.
Original concept of the series by Maria Isabel Sánchez Vegara, published by Alba Editorial, s.l.u
Produced under trademark licence from Alba Editorial s.l.u and Beautifool Couple S.L.

First Published in the UK in 2018 by Frances Lincoln Children's Books, an imprint of The Quarto Group.
The Old Brewery, 6 Blundell Street, London N7 9BH, United Kingdom.
T (0)20 7700 6700 F (0)20 7700 8066 **www.QuartoKnows.com**
First Published in Spain in 2018 under the title Pequeña & Grande Mother Teresa
by Alba Editorial, s.l.u., Baixada de Sant Miquel, 1, 08002 Barcelona. www.albaeditorial.es
All rights reserved.

A catalogue record for this book is available from the British Library.
ISBN 978-1-78603-290-4

The illustrations were created with gouache, coloured pencils, scanned textures and digital techniques.
Set in Futura BT.

Published by Rachel Williams • Designed by Karissa Santos
Edited by Katy Flint • Production by Jenny Cundill

Manufactured in Guangdong, China CC012021

Photographic acknowledgements (pages 28-29, from left to right) 1. The young Albanian born Anjez Gonxhe Bojaxhiu, with her sister Aga, in
Macedonian traditional costume, c. 1925 © Vittoriano Rastelli / Corbis via Getty Images 2. Mother Teresa of Calcutta, c. 1930 © Vittoriano
Rastelli / Corbis via Getty Images 3. Mother Teresa sighted on October 16, 1971 © Ron Galella / Getty Images 4. Mother Teresa with a child
from the orphanage she operates in Calcutta, 1974 © Nik Wheeler / Sygma via Getty Images

Collect the *Little People*, **BIG DREAMS**® series:

FRIDA KAHLO

COCO CHANEL

MAYA ANGELOU

AMELIA EARHART

AGATHA CHRISTIE

MARIE CURIE

ROSA PARKS

AUDREY HEPBURN

EMMELINE PANKHURST

ELLA FITZGERALD

ADA LOVELACE

JANE AUSTEN

GEORGIA O'KEEFFE

HARRIET TUBMAN

ANNE FRANK

MOTHER TERESA

JOSEPHINE BAKER

L. M. MONTGOMERY

JANE GOODALL

SIMONE DE BEAUVOIR

MUHAMMAD ALI

STEPHEN HAWKING

MARIA MONTESSORI

VIVIENNE WESTWOOD

MAHATMA GANDHI
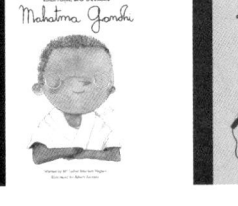

DAVID BOWIE

WILMA RUDOLPH

DOLLY PARTON

BRUCE LEE

RUDOLF NUREYEV

ZAHA HADID

MARY SHELLEY

MARTIN LUTHER KING JR.

DAVID ATTENBOROUGH

ASTRID LINDGREN

EVONNE GOOLAGONG

BOB DYLAN

ALAN TURING

BILLIE JEAN KING

GRETA THUNBERG

JESSE OWENS

JEAN-MICHEL BASQUIAT

ARETHA FRANKLIN

CORAZON AQUINO

PELÉ

ERNEST SHACKLETON

STEVE JOBS

AYRTON SENNA

LOUISE BOURGEOIS

ELTON JOHN

JOHN LENNON

PRINCE

CHARLES DARWIN

CAPTAIN TOM MOORE

HANS CHRISTIAN ANDERSEN

STEVIE WONDER

MEGAN RAPINOE

MARY ANNING

MALALA YOUSAFZAI

ANDY WARHOL

ACTIVITY BOOKS

STICKER ACTIVITY BOOK

COLOURING BOOK

LITTLE ME, BIG DREAMS JOURNAL

Discover more about the series at www.littlepeoplebigdreams.co.uk